Superstars
of
WWE

by Todd Kortemeier

AMICUS HIGH INTEREST • AMICUS INK

Amicus High Interest and Amicus Ink
are imprints of Amicus
P.O. Box 1329, Mankato, MN 56002
www.amicuspublishing.us

Library of Congress Cataloging-in-Publication Data
Names: Kortemeier, Todd, 1986-
Title: Superstars of WWE / by Todd Kortemeier.
Description: Mankato, MN : Amicus High Interest, [2016] | Series: Pro
sports superstars |
Includes bibliographical references and index. | Audience: Grades: K to
Grade 3.
Identifiers: LCCN 2015034791 (print) | LCCN 2015046154 (ebook) |
  ISBN 9781607539438 (hardcover)
  ISBN 9781681510330 (pdf ebook)
  ISBN 9781681521084 (paperback)
Subjects: LCSH: Wrestlers--Biography--Juvenile literature. | World
Wrestling Federation--History--Juvenile literature. | World Wrestling
Entertainment, Inc.--History--Juvenile literature.
Classification: LCC GV1196.A1 K67 2016 (print) | LCC GV1196.A1 (ebook) |
DDC 796.8120922--dc23
LC record available at http://lccn.loc.gov/2015034791

Photo Credits: George Napolitano/FilmMagic/Getty Images, cover, 8–9;
Moses Robinson/Getty Images, 2, 6; Ethan Miller/Getty Images, 5, 12; Don
Feria/AP Images for WWE/AP Images, 11; Jonathan Bachman/AP Images
for WWE/AP Images, 15; Bob Levey/WireImage/Getty Images, 16, 22; Paul
Abell/AP Images for WWE/AP Images, 18–19; JP Yim/Getty Images, 21

Produced for Amicus by The Peterson Publishing Company
and Red Line Editorial.

Editor Arnold Ringstad
Designer Becky Daum

Printed in the United States of America
North Mankato, MN

HC 10 9 8 7 6 5 4 3 2 1
PB 10 9 8 7 6 5 4 3 2 1

TABLE OF CONTENTS

STARS OF THE RING

WWE wrestlers are strong and skilled. Their special moves make crowds cheer. WWE has many stars. Here are some of the best.

"STONE COLD" STEVE AUSTIN

Few wrestlers stood a chance against Steve Austin. He won the **Royal Rumble** three times. The first was in 1997. Austin entered the **Hall of Fame** in 2009.

Austin got his nickname from his wife. One day she made tea. She told him to drink it before it got stone cold.

Johnson has become a movie star.

DWAYNE "THE ROCK" JOHNSON

Dwayne Johnson became "The Rock" in 1998. He was very popular. He was called "The People's Champion." His special move was the Rock Bottom. He won many matches with it.

TRIPLE H

Triple H won the Royal Rumble in 2002. He led teams of wrestlers. In 2011, he traded his wrestling gear for a business suit. He now helps run WWE.

JOHN CENA

John Cena watched wrestling as a kid. He has become one of the top wrestlers. His first match was in 2002. Since then he has won 15 **titles**. Cena is loyal to his fans.

BROCK LESNAR

Brock Lesnar won his first title in 2002. He was just 25 years old. Lesnar did not stop there. He won many more titles. Lesnar won the **heavyweight championship** in 2014. He is still popular today.

Lesnar has also won an MMA championship.

RANDY ORTON

Randy Orton's father and uncle both wrestled. Orton joined WWE in 2002. His main move is the RKO. He leaps into the air. Then he pulls the other fighter to the floor. Orton won the heavyweight championship in 2013.

Orton's father won the first WrestleMania.

SHEAMUS

Sheamus is from Ireland. He has bright red hair. His fans love his fighting style. He joined WWE in 2009. He became **King of the Ring** in 2010. He won the Royal Rumble in 2012.

SETH ROLLINS

Rollins joined WWE in 2012. He formed a team called The Shield. They were hard to stop. Rollins then fought on his own. He won the heavyweight championship in 2015.

WWE has had many great superstars. Who will be next?

Rollins became a pro wrestler at age 17.

WWE FAST FACTS

Headquarters: Stamford, Connecticut

Weekly Shows: 4

Audience: Available in 650 million homes in 25 languages

Average Wrestler Salary: $500,000 per year

Most WWE World Heavyweight Championship Reigns: John Cena, 12 as of February 2016

WORDS TO KNOW

Hall of Fame – a collection of the best wrestlers of all time

heavyweight championship – the highest level of championship in WWE. Wrestlers become the heavyweight champion by defeating the current champion. The time in which a wrestler remains champion is called a reign.

King of the Ring – a wrestling tournament in which wrestlers are eliminated after losing a match; the final winner is called "king of the ring"

MMA – mixed martial arts, a competition in which fighters use many fighting styles

Royal Rumble – a major once-a-year wrestling event in which many wrestlers fight at once

title – a WWE championship victory

WrestleMania – a major, once-a-year wrestling event that features fights between top wrestlers

LEARN MORE

Books
Black, Jake. *The Ultimate Guide to WWE*. New York: Grosset & Dunlap, 2011.

Pantaleo, Steve. *WWE Ultimate Superstar Guide*. Indianapolis, IN: DK/Brady Games, 2015.

Websites
WWE.com
http://www.wwe.com
Learn more about today's top wrestling stars at the official WWE website.

WWE Games and Activities
http://www.wwe.com/play/games
Check out online games based on WWE stars.

INDEX